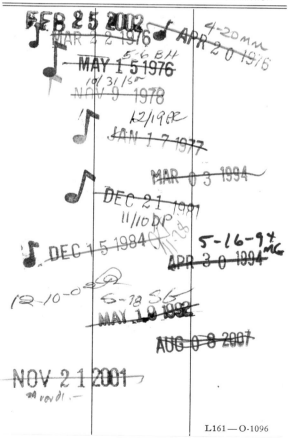

AMERICAN POPULAR MUSIC

The Growing Years, 1800-1900

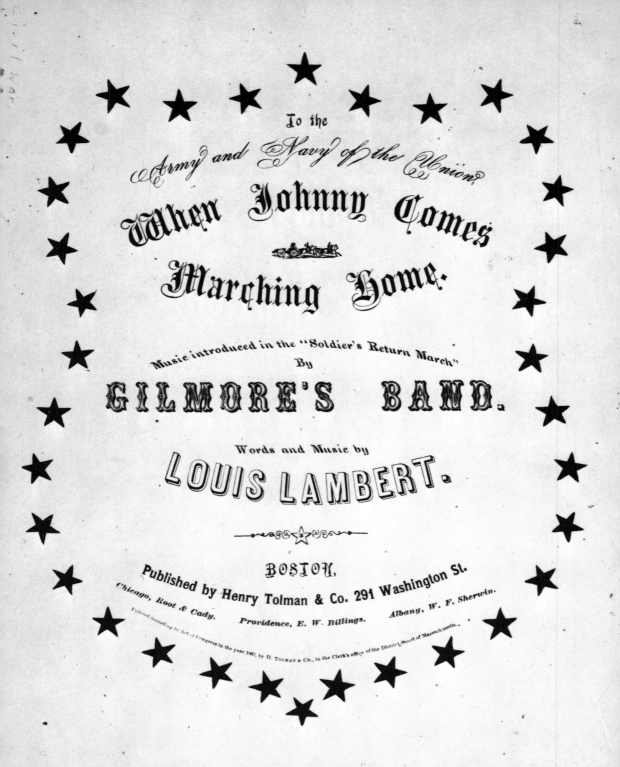

To the
Army and Navy of the Union,

When Johnny Comes
Marching Home.

Music introduced in the "Soldier's Return March"
By

GILMORE'S BAND.

Words and Music by
LOUIS LAMBERT.

BOSTON,
Published by Henry Tolman & Co. 291 Washington St.

Chicago, Root & Cady.   Providence, E. W. Billings.   Albany, W. F. Sherwin.

Entered according to Act of Congress in the year 1863, by H. Tolman & Co., in the Clerk's office of the District Court of Massachusetts.

AMERICAN POPULAR MUSIC

The Growing Years, 1800-1900

Berenice Robinson Morris

Illustrated with photographs

FRANKLIN WATTS, INC.
New York / 1972

For Jeff and Donny

Cover illustration by Rodney Shackell

Library of Congress Cataloging in Publication Data

Morris, Berenice Robinson.
    American popular music.

    SUMMARY: A brief look at the music of nine-
teenth-century America showing how it reflects the
history of a growing nation.
    [1. Music, Popular—History and criticism] 1.
Music—Juvenile literature. 2. Music—U. S.—History
and criticism. I. Title.
ML3930.A2M664   780'.42'0973   77-189760
ISBN 0-531-02567-5

Music

CONTENTS

AMERICAN POPULAR MUSIC

The Growing Years, 1800-1900

AMERICANS
AND THEIR MUSIC

Hard rock, folk rock, soul, and blues,
Country, new country, folk, and jazz.

These are some of the words that come to mind when one thinks of American popular music.

Tijuana Brass, Johnny Cash,
Fifth Dimension, Bob Dylan,
Aretha Franklin, Duke Ellington.

These, too, are names that come to mind when one thinks of American popular music; of *today's* American popular music.

As long as there has been an American people, there has been American popular music. Popular music means music of the people. And Americans have made music at everything they have done. In fact, it has been said that the history of the United States can be traced in the music its people have made.

Would all the music have been the same as that we hear today? No, no more than the life, the people, and the country today are exactly what they were in the past.

Some of the older music still survives. Some of it has been completely forgotten. Some has changed along the way, but still furnishes roots and influences for today's popular music.

Let's take a brief look at the country, the people, and their music in the early part of the nineteenth century when the nation was still young. Let's observe the country through its years of expansion and growth until it became prosperous, strong, and powerful — until finally at the end of the century it became a world power.

AMERICA BY
WHEEL AND BARGE

By the year 1815, America had already fought two wars. The original thirteen states were now eighteen; by 1821, six more states were to come into the Union. Due to treaty settlements and land purchases, the boundaries of the United States now extended from the Atlantic Ocean across the Appalachian Mountains, across the prairies, over the plains, clear to the Rockies.

Many people preferred to remain on farms in the East or in cities near the seacoast. But, almost daily, boatloads of immigrants arrived from abroad. They came from England. They came from Ireland. They came from Germany, Sweden, and other countries. They were driven by persecution, both religious and political. They were also inspired by the hope of finding a good life for themselves and their children in the New World. Thus they undertook the hazardous trip across the ocean. Once in America, many of them joined Americans in the trek west.

The land was there and waiting, but the problem was how to get to it.

First, the pioneers traveled the coastal waters and rivers as far as they were navigable, by boat and raft.

Then roads had to be built, for the horseback trails were not wide enough to accommodate the increasingly large covered wagons (called Conestoga wagons) that were used. These wagons carried not only the people, but also their household goods. Often they served as temporary homes, as do the mobile homes of the present day.

Some of the roads were constructed of rough logs laid side

Pioneers traveling west in Conestoga wagons found that the roads were rough and the traveling was slow. Often the pioneers sang to make the time pass more pleasantly.

by side. These were called corduroy roads because they so much resembled that wide-ribbed cotton material.

Recognizing how important roads were in hastening the settling of the West, the federal government finally stepped in and authorized the building of the Cumberland Road, which originally went from Cumberland, Maryland, to Wheeling, on the Ohio River. Later it was to be extended and was generally known as the National Road.

The trips by wagon on the roads leading west could not

have been very comfortable. Traveling was slow and monotonous. Often the travelers sang to pass the time. Sometimes they accompanied themselves by banjo or fiddle. Here are the words of one song, called "Cumberland Gap." (Daniel Boone had marked out an old Indian wilderness trail through Cumberland Gap in 1775.)

Lay down, boys, take a little nap,
We're all going down to Cumberland Gap.
Chorus:
Cumberland Gap, Cumberland Gap,
We're all going down to Cumberland Gap.

Me and my wife, my wife Pat,
We all live down to Cumberland Gap.
(Chorus)

Cumberland Gap, it ain't very fur,
It's just three miles from Middlesboro.
(Chorus)

Another song that is sometimes still sung today was,

THE OLD GRAY MARE

The old gray mare, she ain't what she used to be,
Ain't what she used to be, ain't what she used to be.
The old gray mare, she ain't what she used to be,
    Many long years ago.
Chorus:
Many long years ago, many long years ago,
The old gray mare, she ain't what she used to be,
    Many long years ago.

[4]

The old gray mare she kicked on the whiffletree,
Kicked on the whiffletree, kicked on the whiffletree,
The old gray mare she kicked on the whiffletree,
    Many long years ago.
(Chorus)

About every twelve miles along the road, an inn or a tavern
was built. Here the wagoners could feed and rest their horses.
The weary travelers could also relax and, of course, get supper.
Whiskey flowed freely (at three cents a glass) and the evenings
often became very gay. Many of the innkeepers played a good
fiddle, and the songs and dancing could be very lively.

One of the favorites that has come down to us is "Turkey in
the Straw." The tune is an old one, brought over from abroad,
probably from Ireland, but there are many different versions of
the words.

As I was a-gwine down the road,
Tired team and a heavy load,
Crack my whip and the leader sprung;
I says day-day to the wagon tongue.
Chorus:
Turkey in the straw, turkey in the hay,
Roll 'em up and twist 'em up a high tuckahaw,
And hit 'em up a tune called Turkey in the Straw.

Went out to milk and I didn't know how,
I milked the goat instead of the cow.
A monkey sittin' on a pile of straw
A-winkin' at his mother-in-law.
(Chorus)

[5]

Met Mr. Catfish comin' downstream,
Says Mr. Catfish, "What does you mean?"
Caught Mr. Catfish by the snout
And turned Mr. Catfish wrong side out.
(Chorus)

Came to the river and I couldn't get across,
Paid five dollars for an old blind hoss,
Wouldn't go ahead, nor he wouldn't stand still,
So he went up and down like an old sawmill.
(Chorus)

As I came down the new cut road,
Met Mr. Bullfrog, met Miss Toad,
And every time Miss Toad would sing,
Ole Bullfrog cut a pigeon wing.
(Chorus)

Oh, I jumped in the seat, and I gave a little yell,
The horses run away, broke the wagon all to hell;
Sugar in the gourd and honey in the horn,
I never was so happy since the hour I was born.
(Chorus)

THE CANALS

A great event took place in 1825. The Erie Canal was finally finished. Now it was possible to travel uninterruptedly by water from New York to Albany, by way of the Hudson River, and then by canal to Buffalo and the Great Lakes. The canal barges were hauled by mules who plodded along paths beside the waterway. The barges were tied to the mules (usually one mule at the front of the barge and one at the rear).

Many ballads were sung about the Erie Canal. Here is one that still survives.

THE ERIE CANAL

I've got a mule, her name is Sal,
Fifteen miles on the Erie Canal.
She's a good old worker and a good old pal,
Fifteen miles on the Erie Canal.
We've hauled some barges in our day,
Filled with lumber, coal, and hay,
And we know every inch of the way
From Albany to Buffalo.
Chorus:
Low bridge, ev'rybody down!
Low bridge, for we're comin' to a town!
And you'll always know your neighbor,
You'll always know your pal,
If you ever navigated on the Erie Canal.

[7]

An early engraving of the Erie Canal. In the background is a barge, hauled by mules plodding along the towpath. Many ballads were sung about the Erie Canal. (Charles Phelps Cushing)

THE STEAMBOATS

In August, 1807, the first boat driven by a steam engine success-
fully made the journey up the Hudson River from New York to
Albany and back to New York. Her name was the *Clermont*
and her designer was Robert Fulton. The trip took three days
in actual running time — five days, with stops.

Now boats could travel upstream against the current,
whereas previously they had floated downstream on inland
rivers like the Ohio and were usually abandoned at the end of
their downriver journey. Steamboats were constantly improved,
and by 1825 they could go upstream as rapidly as sixteen miles
an hour, downstream at twenty-five to thirty miles.

At Albany, passengers and freight had to transfer to barges
drawn by horses, for the Erie Canal was too narrow for steamboats. At Buffalo, transfer was made again to steamboats, either
to go across the Great Lakes or to connect by lake and then barge
and canal with the Ohio River. From the Ohio, it was possible
to go by steamboat down the Mississippi, clear to New Orleans.
By similar connections the return voyage was made from New
Orleans to New York. In time, some of the steamboats, especially those on the Mississippi, were built luxuriously, and they
kept their popularity with passengers for many years, long after
the railroads were built. In 1971, the well-known *Delta Queen*,
completely rehabilitated at a cost of several million dollars,
started to make the run again from New Orleans.

There were many races between the steamboats, not only
because steamboat racing was a popular sport, but also because
the first boat to tie up at a river port would gather up most of

the passengers and freight. The most famous river steamboat race took place on the Mississippi in July, 1870, between the *Natchez* and the *Robert E. Lee*. The *Natchez* was commanded by Captain Leathers, while the *Robert E. Lee* was commanded by Captain Cannon. The boats started at New Orleans and docked at St. Louis. So determined were both captains to win that they made every effort to get the fastest possible speed from their boats. Crowds lined the banks of the river to watch the race. As the boats passed, fireworks and cannon were shot off. Despite all sorts of obstacles, including a dense fog that blanketed the river on the final night of the race, the *Robert E. Lee* came in as winner.

Called by newspapers the sports event of the century, the race is still famous and is still frequently heard of in song.

> We are waiting on the levee for the two steamboats to come round;
> We think they're racing hot fired; we think they're loaded down;
> We hear those steamboat whistles, blowing clear and free,
> We're sure they are the *Natchez* and the *Robert E. Lee*.

Opposite, above: Robert Fulton's steamboat the Clermont *chugging her way up the Hudson River. The invention of the steamboat prompted many new songs. (Charles Phelps Cushing)*

Opposite, below: a midnight race between two riverboats on the Mississippi is pictured in an old lithograph. The boat on the left is the Natchez, *famed in song for her race with the* Robert E. Lee. *(Charles Phelps Cushing)*

THE RAILROADS

Just as the canals inspired songs and ballads, so did the railroads. The steam-driven locomotive came into widespread use in the 1830s, but at first the railroad lines ran for short distances only. It was hard to find laborers to do the backbreaking work of clearing the way and laying the tracks. But starvation in Ireland drove thousands of Irishmen to American shores, and many became railroad workers.

"Paddy Works on the Railway" was sung by and about the Irish laborers on the railroads.

In eighteen hundred and forty-one,
I put my corduroy breeches on,
Put my corduroy breeches on,
To work upon the railway.
Chorus:
Fil i me oo ree eye ri ay,
Fil i me oo ree eye ri ay,
Fil i me oo ree eye ri ay,
To work upon the railway.

In eighteen hundred and forty-two,
I left the old world for the new,
Bad cess to the luck that brought me through
To work upon the railway.
(Chorus)

In eighteen hundred and forty-three,
'Twas then I met sweet Biddy MacGhee,

[12]

An elegant wife she's been to me
While working on the railway.
(*Chorus*)

In eighteen hundred and forty-five,
I thought myself more dead than alive,
I thought myself more dead than alive
While working on the railway.
(*Chorus*)

It's "Pat, do this," and "Pat, do that,"
Without a stocking or cravat,
Nothing but an old straw hat
While Pat worked on the railway.
(*Chorus*)

In eighteen hundred and forty-seven,
Sweet Biddy MacGhee, she went to heaven,
If she left one kid, she left eleven,
To work upon the railway.
(*Chorus*)

Here is a verse of another railroad workers' song, still often sung today.

I've been working on the railroad
    All the livelong day,
I've been working on the railroad
    To pass the time away.
Don't you hear the whistle blowing
    So early in the morn?
Don't you hear the captain shouting,
    "Dinah, blow your horn"?

[13]

(Dinah was the name the captain gave the locomotive.)

Almost nine thousand miles of track had been laid in the twenty years since 1830, and that figure went up threefold by the eve of the Civil War. Still, more railroads were needed. As a result of the Mexican War and the settlement of the dispute with Great Britain over Oregon, the United States stretched from the Atlantic to the Pacific.

There was talk and plans of railroads that would span the continent from coast to coast. But only after the Civil War was it possible to complete work on the main lines.

One song was widely sung while the railroad workers were rushing to push the Union Pacific westward and the Central Pacific eastward until, in May, 1869, they were joined in Utah, a territory that had been settled by a religious sect called the Mormons.

THE RAILROAD CARS ARE COMING

The Great Pacific Railway,
For California, hail!
Bring on the locomotive,
Lay down the iron rail.
Across the rolling prairies,
'Mid mountain peaks so grand,
The railroad cars are steaming, gleaming, through Mormon
    land;
The railroad cars are speeding, fleeting, through Mormon
    land.

Many legends grew up about the workers on the railroads. One of the most famous told the story of a black man named John Henry. He was a steel driller and his physical strength was

[14]

Pushing the railroads west across the Great Plains in the days of the covered wagon. In the background, workers lay the rails. Many railroad songs resulted from this new means of transportation. (Charles Phelps Cushing)

A railroad train travels on a single track across the plains.
(Charles Phelps Cushing)

extraordinary. He was so strong that he was sure he could match himself against a steam drill. A contest between the man and the machine did take place in Big Bend Tunnel, West Virginia. John Henry won, but the effort was so great he burst a blood vessel and died.

THE BALLAD OF JOHN HENRY

John Henry said to his captain,
"A man ain't nothing but a man.
An' before I'll let that steam drill beat me down,
I'll die with the hammer in my hand,
Lawd, Lawd! Die with the hammer in my hand!"

John Henry got a thirty-pound hammer,
Beside the steam drill he did stand.
He beat that steam drill three inches down,
An' died with his hammer in his hand,
Lawd, Lawd! Died with his hammer in his hand.

They took John Henry to the graveyard
An' they buried him in the sand,
An' ev'ry locomotive come roarin' by
Says, "Dere lays a steel-drivin' man,
Lawd, Lawd! Dere lays a steel-drivin' man."

The most famous of all railroad ballads is "Casey Jones." The story it tells is true, and it is included here even though it actually took place in 1906.

Casey was a big man, six feet four and one-half inches tall, handsome, "with a heart as big as his body." He had a reputation among railroad men as a top locomotive engineer. Casey drove the crack Cannonball Express of the Illinois Central line from

Memphis, Tennessee, to Canton, Missouri. Everyone recognized Casey's locomotive whistle as he went by.

On the night of the fatal accident, Casey had just completed his run into Memphis and was ready to go home. But the engineer who was to take the train farther was ill, and Casey offered to take his place.

Come, all you rounders, if you want to hear
A story 'bout a brave engineer.
Casey Jones was the rounder's name,
On a six-eight wheeler, boys, he won fame.
The caller called Casey at a half-past four,
Kissed his wife at the station door,
Mounted to the cab with his orders in his hand
And he took his farewell trip to that promised land.
Chorus:
Casey Jones mounted to the cab,
Casey Jones, with his orders in his hand,
Casey Jones, mounted to the cab,
And he took his farewell trip to the promised land.

"Put in your water and shovel in your coal,
Put your head out the window, watch them drivers roll,
I'll run her till she leaves the rail,
'Cause I'm eight hours late with that western mail."
He looked at his watch and his watch was slow,
He looked at the water and the water was low,
He turned to the fireman and then he said,
"We're goin' to reach Frisco, but we'll all be dead."
(Chorus)

Casey pulled up that Reno Hill,
He tooted for the crossing with an awful shrill,

The switchman knew by the engine's moans
That the man at the throttle was Casey Jones.
He pulled up within two miles of the place.
Number Four stared him right in the face.
He turned to the fireman, said, "Boy, you better jump,
'Cause there's two locomotives that's a-goin' to bump."
Chorus:
Casey Jones, two locomotives,
Casey Jones, that's a-goin' to bump,
Casey Jones, two locomotives,
"There's two locomotives that's a-goin' to bump."

Casey said just before he died,
"There's two more roads that I'd like to ride."
The fireman said, "What could they be?"
"The Southern Pacific and the Santa Fe."
Mrs. Casey sat on her bed a-sighin',
Just received a message that Casey was dyin'.
Said, "Go to bed, children, and hush your cryin',
'Cause you've got another papa on the Salt Lake Line."
Chorus:
Mrs. Casey Jones, got another papa,
Mrs. Casey Jones, on that Salt Lake Line,
Mrs. Casey Jones, got another papa,
"And you've got another papa on the Salt Lake Line."

THE GOLD RUSH

Gold was discovered in California! In 1848, more than twenty years before the transcontinental railroad was completed, the magic word "gold" flashed across the country. An employee of a sawmill not far from Sacramento had discovered some shiny yellow particles in the tailrace of the mill. Almost overnight, California was transformed from the quiet, sleepy territory that it had been under Mexican rule to a bustling, booming region that had just been acquired by the United States as a result of its victorious war with Mexico. The picture of a peaceful, charming world that quickly disappeared was preserved in the popular song "Juanita."

> Soft o'er the fountain,
> Lingering falls the southern moon;
> Far o'er the mountain,
> Breaks the day too soon.
> In thy dark eyes' splendor,
> Where the warm light loves to dwell,
> Weary looks, yet tender,
> Speak their fond farewell.
> *Chorus:*
> Nita! Juanita!
> Ask thy soul if we should part.
> Nita! Juanita!
> Lean thou on my heart.

The bustling California of the gold rush is captured in another popular song of the time, "The Banks of Sacramento."

[20]

Ho, boys, ho! for California, O!
There's plenty of gold, so I've been told,
On the banks of Sacramento.

Ho, boys, ho! for California, O!
There's plenty of bones, so I've been told,
On the banks of Sacramento.

Now a great horde of people bent on getting rich quick pulled up stakes and made their way to the West Coast. More than twenty-five thousand emigrants traveling by sea reached California by the end of the year 1849. The trip was long and hazardous, south on the Atlantic, past South America, around Cape Horn, then north on the Pacific to San Francisco — or, a

Gold seekers found the trip around the Horn to California a long, rough, and dangerous one. Many songs came from this experience. (Charles Phelps Cushing)

shorter trip than around Cape Horn, across the Isthmus of
Panama from the Atlantic to the Pacific. To the tune of "Pop
Goes the Weasel," the gold seekers sang,

A Ripping Trip

You go aboard of a leaky boat,
   And sail for San Francisco;
You've got to jump to keep her afloat,
   You have *that,* by jingo.
The engine soon begins to squeak,
   But nary a thing to oil her;
Impossible to stop the leak,
   Rip goes the boiler.

The captain on the promenade,
   Looking very savage;
Steward and the cabin maid
   Fighting 'bout a cabbage;
All about the cabin floor,
   Passengers lie seasick —
Steamer's bound to go ashore —
   Rip goes the physic!

Cholera begins to rage,
   A few have got the scurvy;
Chickens dying in their cage —
   Steerage topsy-turvy.
When you get to Panama,
   Greasers want a back-load;
Officers begin to jaw —
   Rip goes the railroad!

When home, you'll tell an awful tale,

And always will be thinking
How long you had to pump and bail,
    To keep the tub from sinking.
Of course, you'll take a glass of gin,
    'Twill make you feel so funny;
Some city sharp will rope you in —
    Rip goes your money!

To the tune of Stephen Foster's "Oh! Susanna," California-bound travelers sang,

OH, CALIFORNIA

I came from Salem City,
With my washbowl on my knee,
I'm going to California,
The gold dust for to see.
It rained all night the day I left,
The weather it was dry,
The sun so hot I froze to death,
Oh, brothers, don't you cry!
Chorus:
Oh, California,
That's the land for me!
I'm bound for San Francisco
With my washbowl on my knee.

I jumped aboard the 'Liza ship
And traveled on the sea,
And every time I thought of home
I wished it wasn't me!
The vessel reared like any horse
That had of oats a wealth;

[23]

I found it wouldn't throw me, so
I thought I'd throw myself!
(*Chorus*)

I soon shall be in Frisco,
And there I'll look around,
And when I see the gold lumps there,
I'll pick them off the ground.
I'll scrape the mountains clean, my boys,
I'll drain the rivers dry,
A pocketful of rocks bring home —
So, brothers, don't you cry!

Fifty thousand more emigrants, having reached the Mississippi or the Missouri by train and boat, joined covered-wagon trains and first crossed the plains, then moved through the high passes of the Rockies. They faced freezing weather, dangerous diseases, and hostile Indians, but the lure of gold made them push on.

Arrival of the Greenhorn

I've just got in across the plains, I'm poorer than a snail.
My mules all died, but poor old Clip I pulled in by the tail;
I fed him last at Chimney Rock, that's where the grass gave
     out,
I'm proud to tell, we stood it well, along the Truckee route.
But I am very weak and lean, though I started plump and
     fat.

Opposite: gold seekers panning for gold in California. "I'll scrape the mountains clean, my boys, I'll drain the rivers dry." (Charles Phelps Cushing)

[25]

How I wish I had the gold machine, I left back on the
     Platte!
And a pair of striped bedtick pants, my Sally made for me
To wear while digging after gold; and when I left says she,
"Here, take the laudanum with you, Sam, to check the
     diaree."

From Salt Lake City the traveler moved on across the desert
through Nevada, and then to his destination:

When I got to Sacramento, I got on a little tight,
I lodged aboard the prison brig, one-half a day and night;
I vamoosed when I got ashore, went to the northern mines,
There found the saying very true, "All is not gold that
     shines."
I dug, and packed, and chopped. I've drifted night and day,
And I haven't struck a single lead, that would me wages
     pay,
At home they think we ought to have gold on our cabin
     shelves,
Wear high-heeled boots, well-blacked, instead of rubbers,
     Number Twelves;
But let them come and try it, till they satisfy themselves.

In short, all was not gold that glittered, although some men
made great fortunes.

PRESIDENTIAL
CAMPAIGN SONGS

From the time of Andrew Jackson's two campaigns in 1828 and 1832, the American people became enormously interested in national politics and presidential elections. There was no radio or television in those days, and no movies. The only way to become acquainted with the candidates was to go to hear them speak. Many famous rallies and great debates took place. There were torchlight processions and bonfires, and, above all, campaign songs.

In Jackson's first campaign something new appeared on the political scene — the campaign glee club. Pretty girls sang around hickory poles raised by idolators of Jackson, who was sometimes known as Old Hickory.

> Here's health to the heroes who fought
> And conquered in Liberty's cause;
> Here's health to Old Andy who could not be bought
> To favor aristocrat laws.

Jackson's powerful personality and his measures aroused an enraged and diverse opposition. Capitalists hated him for his bank policy. Manufacturers disliked his tariff policy. His efforts to rouse "the humble members of society" against "the rich and powerful" disturbed many Southerners, especially planters fearful of the backwoods farmers' desire for equality. South Carolinians sharply opposed Jackson because he had talked of "suppressing insurrection" among them and hanging "traitors."

The year 1840 saw the first campaign where two truly nationally organized parties were pitted against each other in a presidential election. The Democrats nominated the incumbent President Martin Van Buren of New York State. They could not agree on a vice-presidential candidate and left his choice to the state electors.

Van Buren was a shrewd politician, but he had made many enemies. They said that he was vain and that he was fond of living in luxury. Some of the nicknames they gave him were the Flying Dutchman, the Red Fox of Kinderhook (the town from which he came), and the Little Magician. Worst of all, they blamed him for the severe business depression of 1837.

The Whigs nominated William Henry Harrison, a former territorial governor, whose chief claim to fame was his defeat of the Shawnee Indians in the Battle of Tippecanoe in 1811. Harrison's running mate was a disgruntled Virginia Democrat named John Tyler.

Even though Harrison was a man of comfortable circumstances who lived in a white mansion in Ohio, his campaign managers presented him to the public as a frontiersman, brought up in a log cabin and extremely fond of hard cider. As the campaign heated up, portable log cabins, coonskins, and barrels of cider appeared everywhere.

Here is one song that came out of Whig headquarters.

Let Van from his coolers of silver drink wine
And lounge on his cushioned settee.
Our man on his buckeye bench can recline
Content with hard cider is he!

And another,

An early political torchlight procession in the 1800s. Political campaigning was the inspiration for many popular American songs. (Brown Brothers)

A *"Tippecanoe, and Tyler, too" procession assembles at Whig headquarters. On the side of the wagon is a painting of a log cabin; on the back is a barrel of cider. (Brown Brothers)*

> Tippecanoe, and Tyler, too!
> Tippecanoe, and Tyler, too!
> And with them we'll beat Van, Van, Van.
> Old Van is a used-up man.

The Whigs won, and Harrison and Tyler were elected. But within a month after taking office, Harrison died of pneumonia. John Tyler, a Democrat, became President.

REVIVALS AND
CAMP MEETINGS

Give me that old-time religion,
Give me that old-time religion,
Give me that old-time religion;
It's good enough for me.

It was good for our fathers,
It was good for our fathers,
It was good for our fathers;
It's good enough for me.

It was good for our mothers,
It was good for our mothers,
It was good for our mothers;
It's good enough for me.

It will take us all to heaven,
It will take us all to heaven,
It will take us all to heaven;
It's good enough for me.

At the end of the nineteenth century this was one of the most popular religious songs, especially among the people of the prairies and the plains. Such folks still flocked to religious revivals and camp meetings. These gatherings had their beginnings more than a century earlier. As the frontiers were gradually extended, many wandering preachers rode from settlement to settlement bringing the gospel and "saving souls." When they found they could not reach enough people by personal visits, they arranged camp meetings, large congregations in the open air to which the people brought provisions and where they often stayed for several days. As many as ten thousand people at a time often drove from all over the county to hear preachers of the various sects. Frontier life was hard and lonely, and these meetings filled a great social need as well as a religious one.

The religious frenzy of these meetings proved contagious. The singing rose to a mighty volume. The audience shouted, jerked, danced, and fell to the earth. Some people even went into a swoon and had to be carried away.

The preacher would sing out:

Oh, brethren, will you meet me
   in Canaan's happy land?

And the crowd, answering, would burst into song:

By the grace of God we'll meet you
   in Canaan's happy land.

There were many sects and many songs. One of the strictest sects was the Shakers, a group that originally was an offshoot of the Quakers. One of the loveliest of their songs was "The Gift to Be Simple," a tune the contemporary American composer Aaron Copland used in the ballet *Appalachian Spring*, which he wrote for the distinguished dancer Martha Graham and her company.

Opposite: open-air camp meetings combined religion and sociability. Singing was an important activity at these meetings. (The Bettmann Archive)

'Tis the gift to be simple,
　'Tis the gift to be free.
'Tis the gift to come down
　Where we ought to be,
And when we find ourselves
　In the place just right,
'Twill be in the valley
　Of love and delight.
When true simplicity is gained,
　To bow and to bend we shan't be ashamed,
To turn, turn will be our delight
　Till by turning, turning we come round right.

WOMEN'S LIB

Women's lib! Recently there has been a great hue and cry about it. Articles have appeared in magazines. Books have been written about it. There have been meetings and boycotts to protest inequalities and unfairness in the treatment of women.

Today women want to be treated in almost every way the same as men. They want equal opportunities socially and professionally. They want the right to be considered on merit for important positions regardless of their sex. They want equal pay.

The nineteenth century witnessed the beginnings of a vigorous women's-rights movement. Women actively embraced the cause, and many popular songs were written about their activities. One must bear in mind that life for women in those days was difficult. Before the invention of the stove, women cooked over the fireplace. Before there was running water piped into the house, they hauled it from the well. Before there were sewing machines, they sewed clothes by hand for their families. Often they worked in the fields. Bringing up healthy children was in itself no light task before the discoveries of vaccines and vitamins and the many modern preventives for the diseases of childhood. Not until well into the nineteenth century were colleges established to which women could go to acquire a higher education. And not until much later were women admitted to the professional schools of universities where they could learn to become doctors, lawyers, or engineers.

Perhaps worst of all, they could not vote.

Prominent in the cause of women's rights were such famous women as Amelia Bloomer, Elizabeth Cady Stanton, and Julia

A contemporary engraving of Amelia Bloomer in the costume she designed.

Ward Howe. Other supporters of women's rights were Mrs. Henry Blackwell, better known by her maiden name of Lucy Stone, which she insisted on using in her professional activities all her married life, with the approval of her husband. But perhaps the most famous of all was Susan B. Anthony. She, like most of the women reformers, was active in a variety of causes such as temperance (the fight against the drinking of hard liquor) and the abolition of slavery.

In 1849, nine years after she was married, Amelia Bloomer founded and edited a magazine, called *The Lily*, which sponsored all these causes. But she became best known for her insistence on the right of women to wear trousers. Up to this time, women had worn tightly corseted dresses that almost touched the floor.

Mrs. Bloomer popularized her costume of full Turkish trousers gathered at the ankle. People began to call her the Bloomer Girl, and to call her trousers "bloomers." Bloomer organizations sprang up all over the United States and even spread to Europe. Composers wrote all sorts of music about bloomers. Scores of bloomer polkas, waltzes, and schottisches were published, and people danced to such music. The covers of the musical scores featured flamboyant pictures of girls wearing bloomers.

Here is a song called "The Bloomer's Complaint," published as "a very pathetic song for the pianoforte."

I wonder how often these men must be told
When a woman a notion once seizes,
However they ridicule, lecture, or scold,
She'll do, after all, as she pleases.
If we take a fancy to alter our dress,
And come out in style, "à la Bloomer,"

[37]

To hear what an outcry they make, I confess
Is putting me quite out of humor.

Bloomers were increasingly popular, but Mrs. Bloomer gave them up when she felt they were distracting people from her more serious causes. Soon ladies switched to hoopskirts and crinolines, in the latest French fashion.

Elizabeth Cady Stanton, a keenly intelligent, driving woman, spearheaded the struggle to obtain the vote for women. In 1863, after Abraham Lincoln had issued his famous Emancipation Proclamation, Susan B. Anthony, Elizabeth Cady Stanton, and many other determined women demanded the vote for all Americans, women as well as men, blacks as well as whites. There followed a period of great agitation, culminating in women's conventions that nominated women as candidates for President and Vice-President. Women even had a building of their own at the Philadelphia Centennial Exposition in 1876. Gains in women's rights were slow but sure. In 1869 the first session of the legislature of the Territory of Wyoming allowed women the right to vote, hold office, and serve on juries. The Territory of Utah followed suit the next year. But it was not until 1920 that the Nineteenth Amendment to the Federal Constitution was ratified, granting suffrage to all women in the United States.

This is how one of the songwriters, Frank Howard, regarded the situation in 1869, when his song "We'll Show You When We Come to Vote" was published.

Opposite: an engraving of the 1800s pictures the women of the Territory of Wyoming casting their ballots at the polls. Many songwriters found women's rights a good topic for their work. (The Bettmann Archive)

Oh, how we suffer, maids and wives,
Although our wants are very slight;
How sad and dreary pass our lives,
Now who can say it's right?
We're snubbed at night and we're snubbed at morn,
And looked upon the same as slaves;
We're treated oft with contempt and scorn,
By the men, the cruel knaves, oh,
Sad is the life of womankind,
Trod under foot we've always been,
But when we vote, you soon will find
That we'll fix these "terrible men."

TEMPERANCE

LITTLE BROWN JUG

My wife and I lived all alone
In a little hut we called our own.
She loved gin and I loved rum,
I tell you we had lots of fun.
Chorus:
Ha, ha, ha, you and me,
Little brown jug, don't I love thee!
Ha, ha, ha, you and me,
Little brown jug, don't I love thee.

Since the beginning of the colonies, hard liquor had been a part of the ordinary man's daily diet. The colonists sold liquor to the Indians, who called it firewater. Rum made from molasses was a profitable colonial export. Many people in colonial times believed drinking alcoholic beverages was healthful — a way of warding off disease and even curing it. George Washington had a taste for Madeira wine and even so Puritan a personality as John Adams drank hard cider before breakfast to get started for the day.

True, church pastors had sharply criticized drunkenness even in colonial times, but early in the nineteenth century its dangers, both social and physical, began to stir strong organized opposition to the use of liquor. In 1836 the state of Massachusetts passed a law preventing the sale of "ardent spirits" in quantities less than fifteen gallons. The legislature thought that

THE ORIGINAL
LITTLE BROWN JUG

SONG and CHORUS

as SUNG by EVERYBODY

Composed and arranged by

BETTA.

NEW YORK
Published by S.T. GORDON 706 Broadway
Entered according to act of Congress A 1869 by S T Gordon in the Clks office of D'C' for S°C° of N Y

having to buy so large an amount would keep people from purchasing liquor.

A clever clockmaker in Dedham, Massachusetts, had the idea of striping a white pig with black and red paint. He got a license to exhibit it, charging four and one-half cents for admission. When it became known that a glass of liquor was given away free with each ticket, the people came in droves.

Here is part of the story told in song.

In Dedham just now they had a great muster,
Which collected people all up in a cluster;
And a terrible time, and what do you think,
To find out a way to get something to drink.

A Yankee came in with Real Nutmeg brand,
Who had sold wooden clocks throughout the land;
And he hit on a plan a little bit slicker,
By which he could furnish the soldiers with liquor.

They would not allow him to sell by the mug
Unless he could furnish a fifteen-barrel jug.
And as folks wouldn't drink in a measure so big,
He got out a license to show a striped pig.

The sign on the tent was "A striped pig to be seen,"
The wonder of Dedham, the four-legged brute.
A four-penny bit they paid to get in
Which piggy paid back in brandy and gin!

In the 1840s and 1850s the fight against the evils of liquor

Opposite: cover of sheet music for "Little Brown Jug." (The Bettmann Archive)

[43]

became more intense. Women as well as men organized temperance groups and campaigned against drinking. A novel called *Ten Nights in a Barroom,* by Timothy Shay Arthur, vividly illustrated the tragedy caused by drunkenness. William Pratt dramatized the novel four years later, and the drama played the length and breadth of the land. Both novel and play had a tremendous impact on the public.

After the Civil War the Ohio Woman's Temperance Crusade, which became the Woman's Christian Temperance Union, was founded. In 1872, for the first time, a Prohibition party nominated a candidate for President of the United States. Here is one of the popular songs of the time, which had been sung in *Ten Nights in a Barroom.*

> Oh, Papa, please, Papa, don't drink anymore.
> It makes you so angry and wild.
> Poor Mama is waiting just out by the door,
> Oh, won't you come home with your child?

It was not until the twentieth century and World War I that the prohibitionists were able to secure the enactment of the Eighteenth Amendment, prohibiting the manufacture, sale, or transportation of alcoholic liquors in the United States. Widely flouted in the 1920s, the amendment was repealed in 1933.

Opposite: a cartoon of 1874 pictures members of the Woman's Christian Temperance Union attempting to persuade the hardened habitués of a saloon to reform. (Brown Brothers)

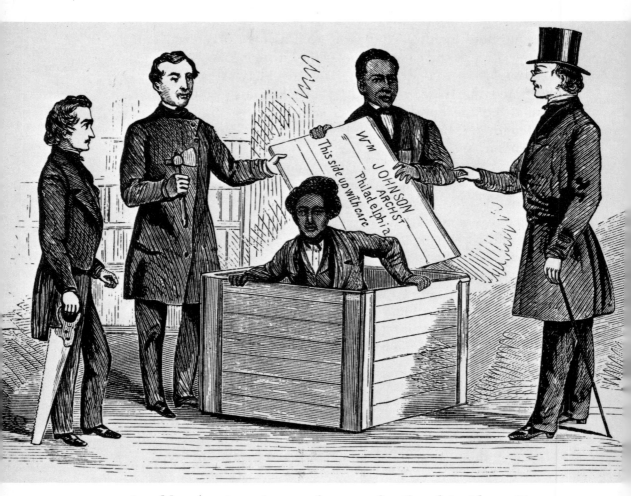

An old engraving of an underground railroad incident. Henry Brown, an escaped slave, was shipped north to Philadelphia in a wooden box and was set free by abolitionists. (The Bettmann Archive)

AMERICA DIVIDED

Perhaps the greatest tragedy of the United States since its founding days has been slavery and its consequences. The first boatload of black people sold into servitude arrived in Virginia in 1619. They were put to work on the tobacco plantations.

During and after the American Revolution, strong sentiment to end slavery sprang up. But in 1793 Eli Whitney invented the cotton gin, and the cotton crop suddenly became very profitable. The plantation owners in the Lower South, where the cotton was grown, needed labor, and slaves were the cheapest and most available kind of work force.

Bitterness grew between many people in the North, who denounced what they considered extreme injustice to the black people, and many Southerners, who came to defend slavery as a positive good. The abolition movement was organized in the North and grew in strength. The underground railroad was set up by abolitionists to help slaves escape to Canada and freedom.

The slave owners of the South resented interference in their affairs by Northerners, and tensions mounted over the extension of slavery into the western territories. The tensions culminated in the Civil War, which broke out in 1861. In 1865, when the southern Confederacy was defeated, slavery was ended throughout the United States by the Thirteenth Amendment to the Constitution. However, the problems created by slavery and the inequalities that the newly freed men, women, and children suffered have continued to trouble us down to the present day.

[47]

BLACK MUSIC

The black people in America, by combining their inherited music from Africa and the musical influences with which they came in contact in America, have created perhaps the most original contribution that the United States has made to music. In it are some of the roots of jazz, pop, folk, and rock.

The first person to write at length about slave music in the nineteenth century was a famous British actress, Fanny Kemble, who had married an American plantation owner, Pierce Butler. In the journal of her life on a Georgia plantation in 1838–1839, she spoke of some of the songs she heard.

One was a work song, sung by the men who rowed her over to the Sea Islands off the coasts of Georgia and South Carolina. They used the song to keep in time as they rowed.

Jenny shook her toe at me.
Jenny gone away.
Hurray, Miss Sukey, hurray!
Jenny gone away.

Miss Sukey was the person in charge of the workers, who had sent naughty Jenny away.

Another slave song, sung in the kitchen, was "Bile dem Cabbage Down."

Bile dem cabbage down,
Bile dem cabbage down,
Work her, gal, don't want no foolin',
Bile dem cabbage down.

[48]

My ole Missus promised me
(Bile dem cabbage down)
When she die, she goin' to set me free
(Bile dem cabbage down).

She lived so long her head got bald
(Bile dem cabbage down).
She gave up idea of dyin' at all
(Bile dem cabbage down).

"Pick a Bale of Cotton" was a work song of the cotton fields.

You got to jump down, turn around, pick a bale of cotton,
Got to jump down, turn around to pick a bale a day.
Chorus:
Lawdy, pick a bale of cotton,
O, Lawdy, pick a bale a day.

Me and my wife can pick a bale of cotton,
Me and my wife can pick a bale a day.
(Chorus)

In the nineteenth century many of the black people were caught up in the revivals that swept the country at this time. The black people identified their hard lot with the various situations of the people in the Bible, and composed songs about them. These songs, which are now called spirituals, served to comfort them.

The story of the rescue of Daniel from the lion's den inspired this song.

Didn't my Lord deliver Daniel, Daniel, Daniel?
Didn't my Lord deliver Daniel?
Then why not every man?

[49]

Old woodcut of a Southern plantation — "pick a bale of cotton."
(The Bettmann Archive)

"Joshua Fit [Fought] the Battle of Jericho" provides a more cheerful note.

Joshua fit the battle of Jericho, Jericho, Jericho,
Joshua fit the battle of Jericho,
And the walls came tumbling down.

You can talk about your King of Gideon,
You can talk about your man of Saul,
But there's none like good old Joshua
At the battle of Jericho.

After the Civil War was over and the black people had gained their freedom, they sang a stirring song to the tune of "Joshua." Two of its verses and the chorus are given here.

Slavery chain is broken at last,
Broken at last, broken at last,
Slavery chain is broken at last,
Going to praise God till I die.
Chorus:
Way up in that valley,
Praying on my knees,
Telling God about my troubles,
And to help me if He please.

Now no more weary traveling,
Because my Jesus set me free,
And there's no more auction block for me
Since He give me liberty.
(Chorus)

[51]

THE CIVIL WAR
SONGS

The tragic conflict between the states inspired the most stirring war songs the United States has ever known. The Civil War was largely a marching war. There were horses and cavalry charges, but the armies were made up mostly of infantrymen. To keep up their spirits, they sang as they marched. Often they were accompanied by marching bands. The men grouped around their campfires at night sang to forget their loneliness and the horrors of the war.

One of the most famous Civil War songs was "Dixie." Daniel Emmett composed it for a minstrel show in 1859. It immediately became a hit, and bands all over the country played it. Emmett was a Northerner and a strong supporter of the Union cause. Imagine his dismay, once the war began, when the Southern soldiers immediately used it as a rallying song for the Confederacy.

Perhaps second only to "Dixie" in popularity in the South was "Maryland! My Maryland," written by James Ryder Randall on April 23, 1861. While teaching in Louisiana, Randall received word of a tragic incident that had taken place in his native city, Baltimore, just a few days before. Soldiers of the Sixth Massachusetts Regiment on their way from Boston to Washington had been marching through Baltimore. Southern sympathizers fired on them and the Union soldiers returned the fire. Three soldiers and nine civilians were killed.

Unable to sleep, Randall sat down and wrote the verses of "Maryland." Jenny Cary, another Baltimorean, adapted them

The armies of the Civil War were made up mostly of infantry-men. As a result, there were many marching songs. Engraving from a picture by Thomas Nast. (Charles Phelps Cushing)

to the German tune, "Oh, Tannenbaum." Having managed to steal through the Union lines to Orange Court House, Virginia, Jenny sang the song on July 4, 1861, for the Confederate troops stationed there. The soldiers were so stirred that they took up the song themselves, finally shouting, "She shall be free. Three cheers and a tiger for Maryland."

> The despot's heel is on thy shore, Maryland! my Maryland!
> His torch is at thy temple door, Maryland! my Maryland!
> Avenge the patriotic gore
> That flecked the streets of Baltimore,
> And be the battle queen of yore,
> Maryland! my Maryland!

And the defiant closing words:

> I hear the distant thunder-hum, Maryland! my Maryland!
> The Old Line's bugle, fife, and drum, Maryland!
>   my Maryland!
> She is not dead, nor deaf, nor dumb —
> Huzza! she spurns the Northern scum!
> She breathes! she burns! she'll come! she'll come!
> Maryland! my Maryland!

"The Bonnie Blue Flag" was another popular Southern marching song. It was originally written for a variety show — this time by a Southerner. Harry Macarthy wrote the words and first sang them to the tune of an old Irish song, "The Jaunting Car," at the Variety Theatre in New Orleans in September, 1861. The song immediately spread like wildfire all over the South. "The Bonnie Blue Flag" was, of course, the flag of the Confederacy.

[54]

We are a band of brothers, and native to the soil,
Fighting for the property we gained by honest toil;
And when our rights were threatened, the cry rose near
and far:
Hurrah for the Bonnie Blue Flag that bears a single star.
Chorus:
Hurrah! Hurrah! for Southern rights, hurrah.
Hurrah for the Bonnie Blue Flag
That bears a single star.

As long as the Union was faithful to her trust,
Like friends and like brothers, kind were we and just;
But now when Northern treachery attempts our rights to
mar,
We hoist on high the Bonnie Blue Flag that bears a single
star.
(Chorus)

After the war was over, Macarthy added these words of
reconciliation with the North:

We're still the "Band of Brothers" that proudly once
unfurled
The Bonnie Blue Flag whose "single star" was sung
throughout the world.
But now that war no longer reigns, let the cry be
heard afar,
Hurrah for *our country's flag*, yes, each and every star.

John Brown, an extreme abolitionist, seized the arsenal at
Harpers Ferry in 1859, while attempting to start a revolt to free
the slaves. He was captured, tried, convicted, and hanged. At

[55]

Sketch from a contemporary magazine of John Brown ascending the scaffold, preparatory to being hanged. One of the lasting songs of the Civil War was inspired by his death. (Charles Phelps Cushing)

once he became a martyr, in the opinion of many Northerners. Thomas Bishop is believed to have written the words below. They were sung to a Sunday school melody of the South. This Union song soon became widely sung.

John Brown's body lies a-mouldering in the grave,
John Brown's body lies a-mouldering in the grave,
John Brown's body lies a-mouldering in the grave,
But his soul goes marching on.
(Chorus)
Glory, glory, hallelujah,
Glory, glory, hallelujah,
Glory, glory, hallelujah,
His soul goes marching on.

He's gone to be a soldier in the Army of the Lord,
His soul goes marching on.
(Chorus)

John Brown's knapsack is strapped upon his back,
His soul goes marching on.
(Chorus)

John Brown died that the slaves might be free,
But his soul goes marching on.
(Chorus)

The stars above in Heaven now are looking kindly down,
On the grave of old John Brown.
(Chorus)

Now for the Union let's give three rousing cheers,
As we go marching on.
Hip, hip, hip, hurrah.

The greatest song to come out of the Civil War — perhaps the greatest of all American songs — was "The Battle Hymn of the Republic." The words of this were written by Julia Ward Howe, the noted author, abolitionist, and fighter for women's rights.

In late 1861, she was invited to a spot outside Washington to a review of the Union troops. Suddenly the troops were called away to defend Northern soldiers in danger from the Confederates. Her return to the city was slow and tedious, for the road was clogged with soldiers and equipment. To while away the time, Mrs. Howe and others in her carriage, including her minister, sang some of the many marching songs, including "John Brown's Body." The minister asked her, "Mrs. Howe, why don't you write some really good words for that stirring tune?"

Very early, in the gray of the next morning, the words came to her mind. Immediately, lest she forget them, she wrote them down on a scrap of paper with the stump of a pencil. These words did not win the $150 prize offered for a national anthem, but Mrs. Howe did receive five dollars when the song was published in the magazine *The Atlantic Monthly* in February, 1862.

Mine eyes have seen the glory of the coming of the Lord:
He is trampling out the vintage where the grapes of wrath
    are stored;
He hath loosed the fateful lightning of His terrible swift
    sword;
    His truth is marching on.

I have seen Him in the watchfires of a hundred circling
    camps;
They have builded Him an altar in the evening dews and
    damps;

I can read His righteous sentence by the dim and flaring
    lamps.
    His day is marching on.

I have read a fiery gospel writ in burnished rows of steel:
"As ye deal with my contemners, so with you my grace shall
    deal;
Let the Hero, born of woman, crush the serpent with His
    heel,
    Since God is marching on.

He has sounded forth the trumpet that shall never call
    retreat;
He is sifting out the hearts of men before His judgment
    seat;
Oh! be swift, my soul, to follow Him! be jubilant, my
    feet!
    Our God is marching on.

One of the most ardent admirers of this song was Chaplain
MacCabe of the One Hundred and Twenty-second Ohio Volun-
teer Infantry. He memorized it immediately upon reading it.
Soon after, he was sent to the front, captured, and held in Libby
Prison in Richmond, Virginia. One night early in July, 1863, a
rumor of a great three-day battle at Gettysburg, Pennsylvania,
came to the hundreds of Union prisoners. They heard that the
Union had met with a terrible defeat. They were frightfully
disheartened.

Suddenly a black man bringing food to the prisoners told
them that the battle had *not* been a defeat for the Union. Instead, it was a defeat for the Confederates. The prisoners were
overwhelmed with joy. Chaplain MacCabe began to sing "Mine

[59]

Julia Ward Howe, composer of "The Battle Hymn of the Republic." (Charles Phelps Cushing)

Abraham Lincoln as President of the United States.

eyes have seen the glory of the coming of the Lord." All the soldiers joined him, jubilantly shouting, "Glory, hallelujah."

Later on, when Chaplain MacCabe had been freed, he spoke in Washington of his experiences. He told of that night in Libby Prison. Again he sang "The Battle Hymn of the Republic." The large audience was so fired with enthusiasm that it sang along with him. When the song was over, far above the noise and excitement could be heard the voice of President Lincoln. Tears streaming down his cheeks, Lincoln asked, "Please, sing it again."

The year 1862 was a succession of discouraging defeats for the Union. President Lincoln asked for three hundred thousand volunteers. Deeply moved, James Sloan Gibbons wrote these inspiring words:

> We are coming, Father Abraham, three hundred thousand more,
> From Mississippi's winding stream and from New England's shore;
> We leave our plows and workshops, our wives and children dear,
> With hearts too full for utterance, with but a silent tear;
> We dare not look behind us, but steadfastly before;
> We are coming, Father Abraham, three hundred thousand more.

President Lincoln's young son Tad took his father to the theater to see an extravaganza called *The Seven Sisters*. In the middle of the performance Tad suddenly disappeared. A few minutes later he reappeared, on the stage, dressed in an army blouse and cap. The President watched his flag-waving young son conduct the entire cast in singing:

[61]

We are coming, Father Abraham, three hundred thousand
  more.

The first black soldiers fought in the Union army in 1862. A
white officer in the First Arkansas [Black] Regiment wrote the
verses of a song that the soldiers of the regiment sang with
enthusiasm to the tune of "John Brown's Body." Its publication
spurred the recruitment of more black troops. Here are two of
its verses.

MARCHING SONG OF THE
FIRST ARKANSAS REGIMENT

Oh, we're the bully soldiers of the "First of Arkansas,"
We are fighting for the Union, we are fighting for the law,
We can hit a Rebel further than a white man ever saw,
As we go marching on.

See there above the center, where the flag is waving bright,
We are going out of slavery; we're bound for freedom's
  light;
We mean to show Jeff Davis how the Africans can fight,
As we go marching on.

A poignant story is told of the hauntingly lovely song "Tenting on the Old Camp Ground," by Walter Kittredge. In the
summer of 1864 some of the troops of the Northern and Southern armies were encamped along opposite banks of the Potomac
River. One hot night the Union soldiers on one side began to
sing the verses of "Tenting on the Old Camp Ground." As the
music floated out over the river, suddenly — almost as an echo
from the other side — came the voices of the Confederates,
joining in the song.

[62]

A Northern company of black soldiers, Company E, 4th Infantry, at Fort Lincoln. Photograph by William Morris Smith, 1865. Black soldiers originated many war songs. (The Bettmann Archive)

We're tenting tonight on the old camp ground,
Give us a song to cheer
Our weary hearts a song of home,
And the friends we love so dear.
Chorus:
Many are the hearts that are weary tonight,
Wishing for the war to cease;
Many are the hearts that are looking for the right
To see the dawn of peace.
Tenting tonight, tenting tonight,
Tenting on the old camp ground.

Not all the Civil War songs were sad. Here are two funny ones. The first is a folk song the black troops loved to sing.

Shoo, Fly, Don't Bother Me

Shoo, fly, don't bother me! Shoo, fly, don't bother me!
Shoo, fly, don't bother me. I belong to Company G.
 I feel, I feel, I feel, I feel like a morning star,
 I feel, I feel, I feel, I feel like a morning star.

The second one, about goober peas, or peanuts, was written by S. Pender.

Sitting by the roadside on a summer day,
Chatting with my messmates, passing time away,
Lying in the shadow underneath the trees,
Goodness, how delicious, eating goober peas!
Chorus:
Peas! Peas! Peas! eating goober peas!
Goodness, how delicious, eating goober peas!

[64]

Just before the battle the general hears a row,
He says, "The Yanks are coming, I hear their rifles now,"
He turns around in wonder, and what do you think he sees?
The Georgia militia eating goober peas!
(Chorus)

"When Johnny Comes Marching Home" was introduced
during the Civil War by Patrick Gilmore, the first outstanding
American bandmaster. In 1869, he organized the enormous
Peace Jubilee, which had an orchestra of one thousand and a
chorus of ten thousand. "When Johnny Comes Marching
Home" was also to become a war song of the Spanish-American
War of 1898. Much more recently the classical composer Roy
Harris utilized it in his overture entitled *When Johnny Comes
Marching Home.*

When Johnny comes marching home again,
Hurrah! Hurrah!
We'll give him a hearty welcome then,
Hurrah! Hurrah!
The men will cheer, the boys will shout,
The ladies they will all turn out,
And we'll all feel gay
When Johnny comes marching home.

AT HOME,
NEAR HOME

After the Civil War the country grew. Daily the improved steamboat service brought hundreds of immigrants from abroad. The sprawling network of railroads that stretched ever longer carried these people to the far reaches of the country. Cities sprang up. Towns grew. Factories were built. Industries were established. The telegraph, the telephone, and the electric light were invented. The United States became a prosperous nation.

Now there was leisure, time, and money for amusement. But it was still long before the day of movies, radio, television, and the automobile. How did people amuse themselves?

Families gathered in the parlor around the piano and sang together. Men dining at their womanless clubs gathered together after dinner and sang. Ladies sang at their quilting bees. And the children sang in school as well as at home.

Back in 1800, an upright piano was built in Philadelphia, and Thomas Jefferson, a good musician as well as a music lover, was "sorely tempted" to buy it for his estate in Monticello. But shortly afterward he moved into the White House and no more was heard from him about the piano.

Pianos had been made in Europe for some time before this, but it was not until the 1840s and 1850s that these instruments were manufactured in quantity in the United States and were sold in large numbers. By the 1870s, no fairly prosperous young couple would consider their home properly furnished without a piano. Often salesmen made a "package deal," selling pianos with sewing machines. Frequently both were advertised together, along with corsets.

Because people were singing and playing musical instruments, they needed sheet music. Music publishing became a flourishing business. Printing methods improved. So did the reproduction of pictures in color. Sheet music could now be sold with boldly colored picture covers advertising the contents within. Many songbooks and collections were printed. Music publishers made fortunes.

Sentimental ballads were very popular in the earlier years of the nineteenth century. Sad songs had more appeal than happy ones. Tragedies of all kinds were set in song: children lost in snowstorms, dying mothers, ships disappearing at sea, fires, train wrecks. Unhappy love affairs were a specialty.

True, sports events and the fashions of the times vied for popularity in song with these tragic events. People sang, too, about city and country life; about current events and politics; and, as we have already seen, there were many work songs and war songs.

"The Snowstorm" was the tale of a distraught wife wandering over the snow-covered mountains with her baby in her arms in search of her husband, already frozen to death. "The Vulture of the Alps" described the agony of a mother whose baby was seized from her arms by a vulture. "The Maniac," by Henry Russell, was a special favorite. Much of its popularity was attributed to the effect it had on audiences when it was sung by a celebrated traveling family troupe, the Hutchinsons.

"The Ship on Fire" was another of Russell's popular hits. This song, with a truly dramatic piano accompaniment, told of a sudden fire on a storm-tossed ship. Eventually the central characters of the ballad — mother, father, and child — were rescued. "Thank God, we're saved!" So ended the song with solemn chords on the piano.

The best of the early sentimental ballads, "Home, Sweet

Home," was written by John Howard Payne in 1823. It is still popular today. The tune, from an operetta for which Payne wrote the libretto — the story and words — is attributed to Sir Henry Rowley Bishop.

'Mid pleasures and palaces though we may roam,
Be it ever so humble, there's no place like home;
A charm from the skies seems to hallow us there,
Which, seek thro' the world, is ne'er met with elsewhere.
Chorus:
Home! Home! Sweet, sweet home!
There's no place like home,
There's no place like home.

An exile from home, splendor dazzles in vain,
Oh, give me my lowly thatched cottage again;
The birds singing gaily, that come at my call;
Give me them, with that peace of mind, dearer than all.
(Chorus)

To thee I'll return, overburdened with care,
The heart's dearest solace will smile on me there.
No more from that cottage again will I roam,
Be it ever so humble, there's no place like home.
(Chorus)

Jenny Lind, the famous "Swedish Nightingale," who was brought to this country by P. T. Barnum of the Barnum and Bailey Circus, sang "Home, Sweet Home" as an encore at a

Opposite: this painting of the 1800s expresses the sentimentality of some of the popular music of the century. (Charles Phelps Cushing)

[69]

concert attended by United States President Millard Fillmore and Daniel Webster. After she had finished the song she turned and pointed to the composer, who was in the hall. The audience gave him a standing ovation.

In 1862, the noted Italian soprano Adelina Patti sang at the White House for President and Mrs. Lincoln. The Lincolns were very sad, for their son Willy had recently died. When Madame Patti asked the President what special song she could sing for them, he replied, "Home, Sweet Home." And when she said she was not sure of the words, Lincoln got the music and placed it on the piano for her. It proved to be the right song at the right moment.

Opposite: John Howard Payne, composer of "Home Sweet Home." (Charles Phelps Cushing)

MINSTREL SHOWS

In 1828, a white man named Thomas Rice played the part of a black field hand in a play in Louisville, Kentucky. In order to do so, he blackened his face with burnt cork. Between the acts he sang a song called "Jim Crow," and he did a dance with it. He was an instantaneous hit. The song became the first American popular song to achieve international success.

Unfortunately, the words "Jim Crow" also came to have an unhappy meaning for the black people, implying racial segregation. This was not the meaning that Rice wished to convey.

This is the story of how the song originated. Rice had seen an old, bent, rheumatic black man working in a stable. He sang to himself and did an odd kind of dance — shuffling and giving a little jump every time he came to the chorus. Rice was enchanted. He sang the song and imitated the dance. This was the first real minstrel song.

JIM CROW

Come, listen, all you girls and boys,
I'm just from Tuckahoe.
I'm going to sing a little song.
My name's Jim Crow.
Wheel about and turn about,
And do just so;
Every time I wheel about,
I jump Jim Crow.

The minstrel show gradually evolved into a pattern. The

first part was a collection of songs, jokes, and patter in black people's dialect. The performers sat in a semicircle. There were two endmen. One was called Mr. Tambo because he played the tambourine. The other was called Mr. Bones because he played the bone castanets. In the middle sat the middle man, who was called Mr. Interlocutor. He was a master of ceremonies.

The second half of the show was called an "olio." This was a mixture — a combination of songs and dances, accompanied by banjo and violin in addition to tambourine and bones. The entire company participated in the finale, the last act. Usually it concluded with a walk-around or a cakewalk — black people's dances.

One of the songs most frequently sung in the minstrel shows was,

ANIMAL FAIR

I went to the animal fair,
The birds and the beasts were there.
The big baboon by the light of the moon
Was combing his auburn hair.
The monkey he got drunk,
And sat on the elephant's trunk,
The elephant sneezed and fell on his knees.
But what became of the monk, the monk?

The vogue for blackface minstrel shows spread rapidly in the 1840s and 1850s. They reached California with the forty-niners. They captivated England and even amused Queen Victoria.

The two outstanding troupes were the Virginia Minstrels and the Christy Minstrels. The Virginia troupe was organized by

[73]

Dan Emmett, who later composed "Dixie." He performed with the minstrels as well as composing their songs. E. F. Christy organized the other troupe. One of America's best-known song composers, Stephen Foster, who composed "Oh! Susanna," "Camptown Races," and "Jeanie with the Light Brown Hair," wrote "Old Folks at Home" for the Christy Minstrels in 1851.

OLD FOLKS AT HOME

Way down upon the Swanee River,
Far, far away,
There's where my heart is turning ever;
There's where the old folks stay.
Up and down the whole creation,
Sadly I roam,
Still longing for the old plantation,
And for the old folks at home.

"Carry Me Back to Old Virginny," another of the best-loved American songs, was written by a black composer named James Bland. He was a graduate of Howard University, where he had studied law, but he wanted desperately to become a member of a minstrel troupe. Despite his great talent as a composer and performer, this was denied to him because of racial prejudice. Although the minstrel troupes performed in blackface and although they exploited the black people's great talent for song and dance, they were white and continued to be white. In 1878,

Opposite: the original title page of the sheet music of one of Stephen Foster's songs, "My Old Kentucky Home, Good Night." (Culver Pictures)

MY OLD KENTUCKY HOME, GOOD NIGHT

FOSTER'S PLANTATION MELODIES

Nº 20

As Sung by

Christy's Minstrels

Nº 18. FAREWELL MY LILLY DEAR.
Nº 19. MASSA'S IN THE COLD GROUND.

Written and composed by

STEPHEN C. FOSTER.

25 Cents nett.

NEW YORK

Published by FIRTH, POND & CO. 1 Franklin Square.

Pittsburgh,
H. KLEBER.

Cleveland,
HOLBROOK & LONG.

St. Louis.
BALMER & WEBER.

heartsick and discouraged, Bland wrote "Carry Me Back to Old Virginny" in one night. The next week it was performed for the first time in Baltimore by the Haverly Minstrels. The audience was overwhelmed, and the song received seven encores.

Eventually Bland went to England, where he performed with a black minstrel troupe. Here he was so successful that the Prince of Wales, later King Edward VII, asked him to give a command performance at Buckingham Palace, the royal residence.

EXTRAVAGANZA,
VAUDEVILLE,
AND BURLESQUE

Three other forms of entertainment for which American composers wrote popular songs sprang from the minstrel show.

The Black Crook, often called the ancestor of musical comedy, was an "extravaganza" produced in New York City in September, 1866. Using the slim thread of a story concerning a "black crook" who "sold his soul to the devil," it was a succession of brilliantly staged and exquisitely costumed scenes. One of them included girls dressed in pink tights, an act which caused a good deal of eyebrow-raising and criticism from the church pulpits. Its great song hit was called "Oh, You Naughty, Naughty Men," and the men loved it.

Vaudeville, from a French word for a popular satirical song, was first performed in Louisville, Kentucky, in 1871. But it was a man named Tony Pastor who was responsible for its popularity. Pastor was a composer, performer, producer, and promoter. To attract the ladies as patrons to his theater, he gave away door prizes — pots, pans, dress patterns, even groceries. Many distinguished performers came from Tony Pastor's stage and so did many popular song hits, among them "Mother Was a Lady" and "The Little Lost Child."

After the Civil War, shows sprang up built on slapstick caricatures of people and things. Using dialects, they poked fun at almost everything. They were called "burlesque" shows. In 1891, *A Trip to Chinatown* was produced. This was the most successful burlesque show of the nineteenth century. After a

[77]

countrywide tour extending an entire year, it had a run of 650 performances in New York City.

"After the Ball," by Charles Harris, is the famous hit that came from this show. When Harris first sang it, the audience yelled and stamped for more than five minutes. John Philip Sousa, the renowned band leader and composer of such marches as "Stars and Stripes Forever" and "Washington Post March," played the song the next year at the Chicago World's Fair. It proved such a sensation that for another ten years Sousa scarcely ever gave a concert without playing it. "After the Ball" in sheet music sold more than five million copies.

Harris wrote the song about an incident he actually witnessed. An engaged young couple quarreled at a ball. Harris watched the weeping young girl leave for home alone.

That night, Harris dashed down on a scrap of paper, "Many a heart is aching after the ball." The next morning he wrote the song.

> After the ball is over,
> After the break of morn,
> After the dancers' leaving,
> After the stars are gone,
> Many a heart is aching,
> If you could read them all;
> Many the hopes that have vanished
> After the ball.

Opposite, above: photograph of a quartet from the chorus of the original production of The Black Crook, *1866. (Charles Phelps Cushing)*
Opposite, below: sheet music for "After the Ball." (The Bettmann Archive)

AMERICA,
A WORLD POWER

In 1898, the United States fought a brief war with Spain. As a result of America's quick victory, Cuba was freed from Spanish rule, while Puerto Rico and the Philippines became American possessions. The United States was now a world power.

Two songs were widely sung at this time. One was the Civil War song, "When Johnny Comes Marching Home." The words of the other song had nothing to do with the war, but this song came to be a favorite marching tune of the soldiers. Teddy Roosevelt's cavalry unit, the Rough Riders, adopted it as their official song.

A HOT TIME
IN THE OLD TOWN

When you hear those bells go ding, ling, ling,
All join round and sweetly you must sing,
And when the verses are through,
In the chorus all join in,
There'll be a hot time in the old town tonight.

By 1900, the United States numbered forty-five states; there had been eighteen back in 1815. During the years between, the country had changed from a weak nation whose potential was not yet recognized by the chief European states to a rich and populous world power. America stood on the threshold of greatness.

The songs its people sang told expressively of the nation's

past and its present and they carried a vision of its future.

Perhaps no songs spoke more eloquently of an idealistic America than two that were composed many years apart. These two songs were "America," whose words were written by Samuel Francis Smith in 1831 and set to the British tune, "God Save the King," and "America, the Beautiful," whose words were written by Katherine Lee Bates in 1895.

AMERICA

My country, 'tis of thee,
Sweet land of liberty,
Of thee I sing;
Land where my fathers died!
Land of the Pilgrims' pride!
From every mountainside
Let freedom ring!

My native country, thee,
Land of the noble free,
Thy name I love;
I love thy rocks and rills,
Thy woods and templed hills,
My heart with rapture thrills,
Like that above.

Let music swell the breeze,
And ring from all the trees,
Sweet freedom's song;
Let mortal tongues awake;
Let all that breathe partake;
Let rocks their silence break,
The sound prolong.

Our fathers' God, to Thee,
Author of liberty,
To Thee we sing;
Long may our land be bright
With freedom's holy light,
Protect us by Thy might,
Great God, our King.

AMERICA THE BEAUTIFUL

O, beautiful for spacious skies,
For amber waves of grain,
For purple mountain majesties
Above the fruited plain!
America! America! God shed His grace on thee,
And crown thy good with brotherhood,
From sea to shining sea.

Opposite: "O, beautiful for spacious skies." (Charles Phelps Cushing)

A LIST
OF SONGBOOKS

Boni, Margaret, and Lloyd, Norman. *The Fireside Book of Favorite American Songs.* New York: Simon & Schuster, Inc., 1952.

——*The Fireside Book of Folk Songs.* New York: Simon & Schuster, Inc., 1947.

Carmer, Carl. *America Sings.* New York: Alfred A. Knopf, Inc., 1950.

Downes, Olin, and Siegmeister, Elie. *A Treasury of American Song.* New York: Alfred A. Knopf, Inc., 1943.

Lloyd, Ruth, and Lloyd, Norman. *American Heritage Songbook.* New York: American Heritage Publishing Co., 1969.

Lomax, John A., and Lomax, Alan. *Folk Song: U.S.A.* New York: Duell, Sloane and Pearce, 1947.

Sandburg, Carl. *An American Songbag.* New York: Harcourt, Brace, 1927.

Silver, Irwin, and Silberman, Jerry. *Songs of the Civil War.* New York: Columbia University Press, 1960.

INDEX

ABOUT THE AUTHOR

Berenice Robinson Morris is a New Yorker, a graduate of Hunter College High School and Hunter College, who received advanced musical education at Curtis Institute of Music, in Philadelphia, and Juilliard Graduate School and Columbia University, in New York. Her published books are *New Songs for New Voices* and *American Popular Music: The Beginning Years*. She has received two Bearns Prizes for her musical compositions and at present is Associate Professor of Music at Long Island University.